Banjaxed

Gráinne Tobin

Muireann at last,
best wishes,
Gráinne Tobin

SUMMER PALACE PRESS

First published in 2002 by

Summer Palace Press
Cladnageeragh, Kilbeg, Kilcar, County Donegal, Ireland

Printed by Nicholson & Bass Ltd.

A catalogue record for this book is available
from the British Library

Printed on Crossbow Elemental Chlorine-Free Paper

ISBN   0   95359 12   7   1

for
Peg and Oliver Tobin

Acknowledgments

Some of the poems in this book have previously appeared in:

Cyphers; Fortnight; HU; Kent and Sussex Poetry Society Competition Anthology (2001); *The Dickens; The Salmon; You Can't Eat Flags for Breakfast* (Belfast 2001); *Word of Mouth* (Belfast 1996).

Biographical Note
Gráinne Tobin was born in Armagh in 1951. She lives in Newcastle, County Down. Having taught for twenty years in the Upper Bann Institute of Further and Higher Education where she was Adult Education Outreach Worker, she now teaches English and Media Studies at Shimna Integrated College. She has been a creative writing facilitator for the Pushkin Prizes Trust, the Northern Ireland Association of Youth Clubs and for the Southern Education and Library Board Youth Service. She has been broadcast on Radio 3 and 4, and is a member of the Word of Mouth poetry collective.

CONTENTS

Abseiling

Null air behind me and the face above
saying it's easy if I'd just lean back,
gripping the rope one-handed, into the void.

Eyes closed, I clutch the paid-out line,
sleep-walk backwards off the vertical,
sustained contrariwise, and fall
into my mother's imagined arms,
sure as an infant of her buoyant force.

These days we're hardly fit for such shenanigans.
Her good hand grips a stick,
she leans on me,
her left side's numb with palsied, useless limbs.
The sinister stroke that cut old ties
between mind and motion
caught her unsteady,
casting off into nothingness.

God Send Sunday

Wakened by Sabbath bells
to the cheerful conspiracy
of unauthorised sex,
she'd throw on the kind of clothes
easily thrown off,
open the fanlit front door
and run out for the papers,
handing warm coins
to the shivering stallholders
at the church gate,
where the massed murmur
echoed through stained glass.

Afterwards they'd lie up on their banks of pillows,
passing back and forth between them
broadsheets promiscuously commingled,
as the packed church released its company
to congregate below their curtained window.

Maybe September

for Carole Evans

1. Party Time

Delighted yo-hoes from the side ward
as she models the creased and outgrown nightie
her baffled husband sent; the kind of thing men do.

Flesh swells through open-work embroidery,
improper as six women's loud-mouthed laughter
picturing Mr Surgeon's morning ward-round.

2. Sealed Brown Envelope

Typing up instructions:
keep clergy out of this,
invite a union speaker,
hire the community hall.

She wants *Bread of Heaven*
chorused by rugby players,
her coffin's pathway lined
with high-stepping Irish dancers,
uilleann pipes for our tears
and later, a fluted reel
to lift us back
out of the dark of her grave.

3. Outpatient

Stumbles in, bloodied as from battle,
holding a gauze pad to the spurting wound
where they botched the shunt,
scorched the blistered skin –
and carrying a daughter's Christmas skateboard
bought between hospital and home.

4. Chemo

She toasts her children in Tamoxifen;
a drunken, helpless nausea pours in.

5. Trying To Connect You

It has never been our policy to issue
disabled motorists' parking discs
merely on a temporary basis. These are reserved
for registered drivers genuinely experiencing
impediments to mobility. Now tell me, what exactly
is the precise nature of this temporary problem?

She grips the mouthpiece. Answers.
I have advanced cancer.

Connected by pulsing cable,
handsets warmed to common body heat,
each contemplates the meaning of *temporary*.
Life, a self-limiting condition.

Well, I'll just have to see what I can do,
says the stranger's voice. *I'll ring you back, okay?*

6. Confinement

Outside the room where she is put to bed
on vivid linen chosen long ago,
phones ring and are at once picked up,
nurses and neighbours pass through muffled doors.

Cradled, she chases sleep, sweats out dark hours
struggling for sense. Beyond the tenderness
of smoothed-out sheets, she labours
towards deliverance, cherished
but alone.

7. Told You So

On that last night
she comes to her friend in a dream,
able to speak and move again, to share
the big hug, the pillowy warmth of skin.

I'm dying, she shrugs, and laughing, they shake
their heads as if to say,
Well, wouldn't you know?
Sure isn't that always the way?

Ppolitical Education 1938

Serge school tunic bloused by soda bread
thieved at midnight out of the convent pantry,
gravid with penny bars of chocolate
smuggled in for the whole class
from TB check-ups at the clinic;
pockets not deep enough to hide
the diary palmed by an outraged nun,
listing nicknames of puddings and teachers.

They made you kneel before the altar,
tell God your shame 'til you believed in it.
At her next visit your mother shunned you.

When the German ambassador came,
all the girls sang *Deutschland Uber Alles*,
saluted, ignorant as a kish o' brogues.
That was the year old Jews licked pavements clean.

The Whole Story

All the women in our family
like to toast their arses at the fire
in a more or less ladylike manner,
enjoying the backstage warmth of it
and the familiar soundtrack from my father,
warning us all to be careful,
citing heredity;
for my mother's mother
set petticoats on fire in 1930
– not once but twice –
day-dreaming by the burning turf,
lifting skirts behind her
until the scorched smell and the smoke
brought my grandfather leaping
to roll my young granny
in her own hearthrug,
smothering curls of flame.

Was it quenching or courting?
Thrown breathless on the floor,
corseted in whalebone and carpet,
did my smouldering foremother
conspire in that solicitous embrace?

Family History

Leaving that evening,
ashamed to be seen,
(the word was out
our house was next to burn)
dismantled cot on the roof-rack,
our children buckled in with lies and kisses,
objects of someone's scorn.
A carnival politeness,
it's not the neighbours' fault.

That last look round the house,
lifting the box of photographs,
insurance policies and the cards
saying Welcome To Your New Baby –
even our fear a cliché.

Woe to them that are with child
the pulpits used to rumble
and blessèd are the paps that never gave suck.
Newsreel refugees on endless roads,
always a woman carrying a baby;
wars and rumours of wars.

To avoid the embarrassment
of meeting our attackers
we went the mountain way.

The roadblock surprised us
in that lonely place.
Police weighed up our load,
address and destination.
Experienced in evasion
they waved us on.

Next morning we came home,
ashamed to be seen unpacking.
Nothing had happened.
The bland day lay about us.
Nothing was ever said.

Since then our lives are portable,
our houses stones.
We keep the children's photographs apart.

Holiday Job

All summer when you were the pigshit-
and-maggot-man at the pork pie factory,
lowering racks of decomposing entrails
into hissing vats of alkaline dip,
I lifted warm dead hens from the overhead line,
stuffed them wet in plastic bags for freezing.

Every day was an ache, and our eyes opened
to lifetimes cheaply sold: Spanish migrants
sending wages home to feed their children,
the former maggot-man blinded by caustic
spilling loose onto his face from a high shelf.
The supervisor talked to me in pidgin,
deceived by my Paddy accent and black foreign hair.
I pieced together theories of labour.

At noon we ran to share our sandwiches,
sitting holding hands on mossy tarmac;
the disused tennis-court where we could hide
in the exotic country of new love.
A thin green snake flowed silently under
wire netting into long grass. You named it
for me: *slow-worm*, a pagan English beast
released from children's books and Beowulf.

Hindsight

The mind's eye like a hand-held camera
fixes unsteadily on pink limestone steps
inlaid with seashells,
rubbed to a concave polish.

A corridor jangling with trousered legs,
a tall chair at the back of the classroom.
I sit up like a good girl,
juggling rolled woollen mittens,
waiting for my father to finish
teaching Apprenticeship Maths
and walk me to the dentist.
The whispered question
makes rows of faces turn to laugh:
Daddy, why are all
these big men going to school?

After the check-up, we go hand in hand
to Woolworth's for a choc-ice with no stick.

One-liners

The doorbell chimes its four suburban notes,
a tall shadow shifts in frosted glass.
In their new house she hardly pauses to wonder
if this might be the one
everybody hopes will never come to them.
Round here, expect a load
of firewood, sacks of spuds for sale,
a neighbour's charity raffle.

The man is smiling hesitantly
under his sepia-tinted moustache.
She looks past him for the farm van
and sees he's one of a pair –
his partner's climbing the steep wet slope
to the houses across the street.
Just as she spots the rebuff not yet uttered
forecast in his eyes (for she has a surfeit of spuds)
he speaks his single line:
I'm canvassing for Sinn Féin in the election.

She's suddenly freezing, as their glances meet.
No, quickly, *I don't approve of violence.*

Banned, he turns back down the path
as civilly as he came,
and she's the one who's sorry
for the prim rejection,
for sending him away in the rain
without exchange or explanation,
for letting him make his own strange sense
of prosperous citizens who think that killing
is a vulgar habit, and trust the courts for justice.

When She Thinks of Sex, She Thinks of Cabbages

Passing the stone arch of the railway bridge
slanted over the narrow road
she's going slowly, minding where she steps
in ankle socks and new brown t-strap sandals,
when she picks up a fan of coloured paper
blown from the train window,
flapping in the dusty hedge.

Her head opens like a lid
to photographs of naked grown-ups
doing things in rooms
she does not recognise.

She raises her eyes from the pages,
beyond hawthorn leaves and rusty gate,
to the big flat field of cabbages –
pictures a baby tucked in
under each green curly globe.

Untimely

for Mary Wall

Every woman had been her best friend;
every man had planned to marry her.
The city church was full as if for Christmas.
We'd journeyed through the frozen dark for hours
to be in time for her,
who had never been early for anyone,
but was not, as prophesied, late
for her own funeral,
having taken only months
to die at thirty-three.

Already there were legends
of how she'd kept us waiting,
exhausted by expectation,
furious, duped, swearing *never again*;
then just appear, unlooked-for as an angel,
ablaze with sequinned apologies,
costumed in excuses so lustrous
it was enough to see her and be dazzled.

The funeral meal was like a wedding breakfast;
the bride, however, absent,
forever awaited,
so that in later years
we're startled by girls glimpsed in the street,
loops of fair hair and long scarves swinging by,
and turn in hope to hear her truant voice
propose some folly:
Ah, come on, sure what's your hurry?
We'll be a long time dead.

The Old Wife's Tale

Is it any wonder I'm nervous,
she says, *he's so unpredictable.*
I'll be out for twenty minutes, says he,
and it could be hours later
he'll return, with a trailer full of bargains, or
the car door sheared off, or
holding a bloodstained flannel
to his squashed nose
after toppling off a neighbour's step
straight onto his poor face.
He doesn't listen to a word I say,
she says, *but sure he needs me here*
to do all his worrying for him.

Lightning Conductor

At the first growl in the sky
she'd be up in the roof-space
for her old university notebooks,
and we'd sit delighted with our storm-tossed mother
around the kitchen table,
calling out seconds between flare and crash,
tearing bindings, matching margins,
cutting nicks and crescents
with forbidden scissors.
A lightning party.

Pinched paper blossomed intricately
into fretted lacework doilies
criss-crossed with the clever handwriting
of a firm young woman:
frosted inky syllogisms, gingerbread Latin,
cursive iced embroidery in purple,
all fed to us children,
thrilled to lick it up. Diverted.

Missing

... my turquoise, I had it of Leah when I was a bachelor.
Shylock

We were learning to walk together,
a three-legged pas-de-deux,
stepping out, finding the fit
of arms around waists,
palms in the packed, live
back pocket of the other's jeans.

At Northgate you stopped to buy me
a painted lead curiosity,
a miniature scarlet devil
galloping bareback on a cross black pig –
only six pre-decimal shillings.
I let you put it like an amulet into my hand,
though well taught
not to take presents from strangers.

Disappeared, stolen or lost
out of my deep suitcase
on the Holyhead boat
the very first time we were parted.
If I still had that keepsake
I might remember it less.

Resistance

Carved names make skin prickle,
bumps rise, as we read whose graves
we're walking over on our holidays.
On limestone or granite
in shady cobbled squares
every village lists its children
dead for France.

Stone cross planted by a vineyard,
miles out of town; who has left red flowers?
Fifty years on, we're tourists here,
driving past a murder.
My atavistic right hand twitches like a dowser's
towards my forehead in the sign of the cross
– God between us and all harm –

but back at home, we won't stare at the flowers
pinned in bunches to the city shopfront,
or wired to the roadside fence
where the crater's filled, the asphalt patched.
We'll lower our eyes and drive on, shivering,
resisting the reflex gesture, or collaborating
in the Ulsterisation of grief.

Rural Retreat

July was worst. A young man pulled a knife
on him one evening after closing time,
the pearly sea light fading, as their roof
shook to the ladders of the bunting squad.

Often at night, they would be loudly jolted
from their deep lovers' sleep by unseen fists
thumping the window-pane beside their bed,
insults in accents not yet understood.

They stuck it out, in disbelief at first.
Still the waves played along the rocky shore,
black guillemots nested in the granite harbour.
Village life takes patience, they were told.

The pounding and the jeering petered out;
soon they put right their house and bought a pram.
Bunting bloomed discreetly each July.
From fear or tact, they spent the Twelfth away.

In time the news was bad. The threats began.
Pregnant, she picked the shards of window glass
out of the toy-box, and arranged to sell.
Not quite intimidation, the policeman said.

Hang Your Clothes on a Hickory Bush

Other mothers clucked to hear you tell me:
Put on your wellingtons, and then
run in the puddles to your heart's content.
You were supposed to say: *Good wee girls*
are not allowed to splash in muck and gutters.

Wading luxuriously through flooded potholes
down a clabbery loanin forty years on,
the cloudy lakelets lapping round my feet,
snug and free inside my stylish wellies,
I'm stopped where I stand, ankle-deep,
thankful for wilderness survival lore
handed from seditious mother to daughter:
Be prudent, brave and blithe, my darling,
when you dander down unapproved roads,
and step well-shod into forbidden waters.

A Prayer for Orinda

Now he's really gone, the mirror shows her age.
Time thickens on windowsills, darkness presses
against plate glass in the treetop house.
Dawns keep coming and she still can't move.

Dried-out eucalyptus blades float like confetti,
parasols and hammocks scorch on timber decks.
Fire hazard signs blink on the well-kept hillside
where fine sequoias stand a thousand years,
invigorated by each passing firestorm,
drought-defiant, drinking the morning fog.

Let the forest breathe for her, its perfumed haze
rise to fill the days' leftover sunlight.
Up in the canopy, walking her flammable rooms,
may she try out her house and claim its view,
contemplate heat-blasted redwood seeds,
set to crack and grow in burnt-out ground.

That Was Then, This Is Now

Daffodils bought from a bucket
on the sleety pavement,
their poke of greengrocer's paper
an inhalation mask
dizzying me back
to that pale bay-windowed room,
your jug of early daffodils
sounding a declaration;
wild gold bells, dusted with pollen,
loud, saturated yellow,
scenting the uncertain light.

Ladies' Night

A dozen women settle round a table,
in the community centre proudly
muralled in red-white-and-blue
scrolls, red hands with daggers.

They unzip winter jackets and wait
for me to give them something
they didn't know they had.
Last week it was the cooking demonstration,

tonight they're getting me, one of the other sort,
the creative writing woman, their guest
in spite of church and politics,
for I am trusted to remember

most hated school. Some never learned to write.
I promise them in these two hours together
we will make a poem
pieced from all our lives.

We lay out scraps of stories on the table,
pregnancies and births – my own tale first,
a fragment from our female comedy
offered in all its colours. One decides

to risk me. She begins:
It was a military hospital,
and I a sergeant's wife.
First births are always hard,

but we sat up for officers' inspection
wearing nighties, with our army-issue babies
in their fish-tank cots beside us,
the sheets perfectly folded.

It seems some password has been spoken.
In married quarters, says another,
we made love on mattresses
still wrapped in polythene

for fear of baby stains. The first three feet
of woodwork could be finger-marked,
but doorsteps must be polished daily
for spot checks, gardens paraded,

army wives always on duty.
Our child was nearly blinded once,
her father on manoeuvres;
they said he'd have to follow

the army or his family. He chose
to love us best. We live here now.
Legitimate targets. And she smiles at me,
over the rag-rug poem

we bind with secrecy,
names, ranks, addresses to be left behind,
remnants of these salvaged lives,
when I return to mine, the other side.

At Kilclief

It is the last time he will hold her.
Under her coffin's weight
a brother's arm braces her lover's shoulder.

His face is marked with grief for all to see.
What matter the watchers now?
Form and ritual guard this privacy.

Bradford-on-Avon, Wiltshire, August 6th

Here is the place.
Where the river runs quietly under the bridge
past weavers' cottages, church and library,
pub garden and swimming baths,
among evening smells of leaves and water,
from the boating steps
they are floating lanterns for Hiroshima.

Silently (for my Irish voice
might tell too much)
I take a home-made lantern,
join the murmuring pilgrims
at the water's edge.
The familiar commonplaces
of their conversation
are respectful, like small talk round a graveside.
There are no speeches or announcements.

But in the thickening dusk,
ceremonially, one by one,
they light their votive candles,
set down thin craft
with paddling fingers
on the calm dark river.
The wind breathes
into the paper sails,
the lanterns glide downstream,
glowing, lit from within
against the darkness,
'til the current carries them
softly out of sight.

I light my candle,
float my lantern
with the rest,
watching some catch
in whorls of water,
flash and twist to ash,
their flames extinguished
like the countless dead.

An Error of Taste

As a boy he constructed a humane mousetrap:
now, weeping, trawled our Armitage Shanks u-bend
recovering evidence for the path lab
with a stainless steel soup ladle from the kitchen
and a Pyrex measuring jug, his catch
our ten-week mite that fell so heavily
away from me without farewell or blessing.

Sacred vessels or household utensils? We knew
scouring and boiling would never be enough.
The best we could do was seal them in plastic
and drop them in the dustbin. You may well say
a cairn under the fuchsias might have been fitter.

My father groaned to hear it on the phone.
I must have sounded flippant. After all,
we'd managed. Good in an emergency,
my darling improvised most lovingly,
knowing for sure how hard it all would be:
not until a breathing child lay warm between us
could we bring ourselves to buy another ladle.

Eight Months Gone

Tower of ivory, house of gold, ark of the covenant ...
Litany of the Blessed Virgin Mary

I am your roof and shelter.
Your accommodation is the best I can offer.
I try to be the perfect host,
remembering your vitamin pills, your afternoon naps.
But now you clumsily pace my body
in these dark hours when everyone's at rest,
ham-fisted, insomniac guest. Give you an inch
and you take a mile. Secretive stranger,
we haven't even been introduced.
I've taken you in on faith.
Not that I grudge you this lodging,
in spite of your disorderly behaviour,
waking me with lurching hiccups,
making your tight roof ripple and stretch,
my muscles strain to hold your restlessness.

One day you'll struggle out into the light,
declare yourself at last.
Meanwhile I propose peaceful coexistence.
Lie gently for a while. Soon we will meet
skin to skin, my fugitive, face to face.

Two Figures in a Landscape

Block in a panorama of mountains,
sheep fields in the middle distance.
Put a grey wash on the sky.
Foreground thorn hedges and a downhill lane
stripped by yesterday's storm,
pitted with potholes, studded with boulders,
where the path became a sudden river
flinging back its rough moraine.

Against the torn-up track
outline a man and a woman
tramping out of perspective,
not holding hands, each separately trying
for a foothold in the broken ground.

Under Donard

I put on the peace like a warm overcoat in the October chill.
John Wilson Foster

Weans happed up against All Souls' Night wind
huddle with their parents' arms around them
where galaxies of District Council stars
glamorously explode above the patient crowd
in reckless fountains and cascades of light,
sparklers displayed on velvet sky and mountain.

Searchlights spin, rockets and Catherine wheels
illuminate the gasping, flinching faces
as they get used to bangs that mean no harm,
and volunteers, smiling in Day-Glo tabards,
collect small change in buckets. Now hold steady
as flying bomblets burst, gunpowder clouds
benignly fall to earth like common incense.

Intimations of Mortality
Lines composed while queueing in the Dublin Passport Office

Two babies are dancing
on the Passport Office floor
and if you ask me they have the right idea,
though of course no one has asked me.
I'm dying for someone to ask me.
We're all dying, here in the Passport Office.

Ladies and gentlemen,
you have before you,
as it were,
the human condition –
a multi-metaphorical extravaganza.

Packed together in silent endurance,
this is solitude
as communal experience –
you know you're going to be here for a while,
and it's going to be tough.
You only have your self,
God knows how much time,
and whatever's in your handbag,
so make what you can of it.

You could even
invent some conversation in the queue –
what have we after all but each other?
Let us dance together
'til our number's called.

Lapsed

Queueing bareheaded
in her tracksuit
at the altar rails,
my friend takes the host
from the sour-pussed priest,
puts it to her mouth,
turns down the aisle
with lidded eyes,
hands loosely joined,
routine decorum no disguise
for her yearning
act of communion.

Voyeur, unbeliever, I
sit shaken by mysteries
unvisited since lace mantillas
veiled wild hair
in the convent chapel.

Megahertz

Driving, cooking, keeping appointments,
changing lanes, chopping and stirring,
can flip an overloaded trip switch
or jam all available frequencies,
as when lights dim and airwaves
fill up with martial music
after a coup,
so news doesn't get through
of the regrettable fracas
at the presidential palace
but you can tell they've taken over
power plants and radio stations
and it's keep-your-head-down time
in the cities and the villages,
'til you don't risk remembering
what you were hoping to hear.

Once in a while, though, interference
interrupts itself, the tuner hits the signal,
the current's back, and I'm receiving me
in my own language, loud and clear.

Passing Chatham

It's got a brown sign on the motorway;
the dockyard's Heritage now.

My father-in-law's fifty-year-old
handmade shipwright's tools
boxed up on garage shelves,
his prentice work still useful
for the bit of DIY.

The day the British closed their coal mines
my car radio was tuned to London.

Clandestine, from the engine-room of state,
BBC tones transmitted names of pits,
deliberate as a roll-call
while a colliery brass band
played out a pride I could not know.

Repetitive Strain Injury

My sister snorted, *Women!*
The packhorses of the world.
All those years of shopping bags and children.

When the baby had colic and
I rocked her every night in aching arms
– shrill pain as elbows stretched –
This is how the rack worked of course,
my sister said.

The day my spine skewed,
I limped to the phone.
Women! my sister hissed.
We should be born with yokes!

Blood Orange

You call them *ruby* now,
though I still don't buy them.

Today's front-page atrocity
detonates visceral memory.

It was the fifties then for a long time.
I had a cardigan of duck-egg blue
embroidered with pink flowers,
rose-hip syrup on the National Health.

I took the orange from my mother's hand,
stared at its rouged skin.
She said, *Blood orange*
is only a name.

Skipping to school between hawthorn hedges,
piercing the pith with my thumb,
I tore apart flecked fibres,
saw the bloodstreaked interior,
stained juice dripping.

My own insides gaped.
I threw the bloody mess into a sheugh.
Something pulpy and horrible
pulled at my crotch,
filled my opened throat with salt.

Costelloe Memorial Chapel, Carrick-on-Shannon

Embossed lead casket bedded under glass;
her remains lodged two years in the convent
while he built this fine private gothic tomb,
lavished the profits of his grocer's trade.

Vigilant through matins, compline, vespers,
did lady nuns brood on putrefaction,
consider lesser neighbours' famine farms,
ponder flesh treasured even in decay?

Better to consecrate one's modest limbs
than *make oneself a sewer for some man.*
Custody of the eyes preserves the soul:
safe keeping here for living brides of Christ.

They'd pray for the repose of their dead guest,
whose body's joyful mysteries he'd lost.
Bedside candles flaming at the altar,
draperies of matrimonial lace.

Egyptian New Potatoes

Dry peaty packing rubs off right away,
leaving lumps of sticky grey Nile silt
for me to scrape off with my nails.
Reflected in the steel basin
a school geography illustration:
fertile river valleys of the world.
Bent-backed workers in baggy cotton,
thin brown fingers lifting spuds for export,
handling this selfsame clay.

First potatoes of the season
steam on a blue dish.
Time for the words we always say:
Go mbeirimid beó ar an ám seo arís –
may we be alive this time next year.
Kerr's Pinks. Comber Blues. Eastern Earlies.

Mrs Cornflakes' Trial Separation

Now they've gone, the house looks odd.
So many doorways, corners, stairs,
and no one calling, wanting an answer.
Like those movies where The Woman Alone
makes the point about freedom, or loss:
the tidied room, where everything
is just as you left it, the thermos
full of saved-up hot water
for your next cup of tea,
one plate, one glass to wash.

On my weekend break from motherhood
I can stay in the garden and write
all day if I want, listening
to birds cheep and window frames
creak in the end-of-summer sun,
imagining a lifetime as a number line
where coloured markers flag up progress.

In youth when autumn came, romantic
with woodsmoky dusks and drifts of golden leaves,
every season was one season nearer
whatever it was you were heading for.
Midlife makes you greedy for the spring.

Family can close too tightly,
itchy like rough wool next the skin:
but when at last I have to leave that too
I'll crave the airy voices, downy cheeks of children,
their banked-up warmth against me, in a house
messy with Lego bricks and felt-tips,
forgetting breakfast cereal curdling on the carpet,
captive mornings I poisoned with complaint.

Bad News from Home

Just to be there would not be enough:
to stop at neighbours' gates and ask,
Have you heard the news? and see their faces
seeing your face.

Behind shop counters, men would shake their heads.
You wouldn't feel like doing anything that day,
maybe just watching tides and the horizon.

Images sent to the world on amateur video
over and over like traditional music,
'til you learn to open your eyes through the whole sequence,
sean-nós, pure pitch with the grace-notes of agony.
The decent lens can scarcely frame or focus.
There's an emptiness in the scattered street
where women wander, talking to the wind,
blood on their faces, looking for each other.
Something universal, yet so much like home,
you want to go over the shock of it again,
not to leave them straying by themselves
in the aching gleam of hospitals, the dimmed cortèges.

Scanning beach news-stands for yesterday's foreign papers,
we're helpless here as we'd be helpless there.
A correspondent interviews survivors:
everyone knows everyone in a place like that.

Awareness Evening

Speeches from the Suits go on for hours
but the girl in the next row
has a wood nymph's neck
fringed with tendrils the colour of bark,
outgrowing last month's smart haircut.
The glossy fur
of her gorgeous olive nape
above the white crochet jacket
invites my palm – ah, only
to lay a hand, as if
to brace that stem against
the pull and snap of the incurious world.

Post Op

That man with the moustache has slit your throat,
left you a coral necklace,
silver links and garnet beading.

Yesterday you wore a square white dressing
pinned to one side,
a bubbling inlaid circlet,
Macha's cloakpin.

Each day they take out more silvering.
Surgical pliers hang from your bedhead.

You sit up reciting limericks.

Ablation Ward

The kind nervous one
sealed into his protective suit
gives you the poisoned cup,
your dose measured in curies.

You put on your old nightshirt
in the room where everything you bring
must be destroyed.
Parts of your body have already been incinerated.
No one may touch you.

Outside, your image moving on a screen:
inside, your bedside locker
sheeted in polythene.

Nurses put down food at the door.
Now you're rockbound in solitary,
governed by the laws of uncertainty.

Read your contaminated book
which will be disposed of later.
Do not think.

After the Miscarriage

in memory of Mary Wall

On the doorstep, Mary.
In her arms a fountain of carnations
washing through the emptied house
with their crimson spice –
and she herself a vision of abundance,
light streaming from her spilling hair,
her face, her smile, so charged with life
we borrow some to keep
for when she's gone.

Lodgers

Laid out all night
on the gas ring's blackened pan
in the chill Utility kitchen:
one box of safety matches,
one iridescent rasher,
one pale egg, rocking.

Heavy faces swivel
at the rasp of rented key
drawn in out of the dark.
Landlord and lady wedged tight as sandbags
on their stiff brown leatherette settee
turn back to suitable TV.

Up steep tunnelled stairs,
past the framed
embroidered tract, promising
Jesus, the unseen guest,
the silent listener
to every conversation:
at last to exhale
behind the barred door;
to tumble, giddy, slide
on the madonna-blue
satin bedspread,
and whisper, just in case.

Now Open on Sundays

Once the wire box is buckled on in front,
the supermarket wheelchair gathers purpose:
pony and trap,
rickshaw,
Roman chariot,
husky sled?

Prowling the wide aisles of possibility,
my mother poses for my camera,
brandishing reins in her gloved good hand.

The length of the dairy counter,
our eager team of invisible dogs
pauses to pant with dripping tongues
and steaming fur by the last goat's cheese,
a present for my father
who saw one in a magazine and asked
where you would get a thing like that.

I keep thinking I'm driving,
she says, although I'm steering,
propelling our explorers' cargo
of foreign cheese, coffee and lilies
past the checkout. Next Sunday,
God willing, we'll try out the rickshaw.

In Which She Recalls Cycling to a Tutorial

It is long ago now and what comes to mind
is the wind that would skin you,
straight from the Caucasus,
nosing your coat for gaps
to get its wolf-teeth into.

Head bent, sore eyes leaking, hair pushed
under a terrible tea-cosy hat,
I leaned on the pedals of the bike
my boyfriend's granda fixed up
because bus fares were high and we were young.
The army-surplus greatcoat gripped my waist,
cycle-clips on cord-flared ankles
kept the spokes clear,
hard rain seeped inside the stitches
of my saddlebag,
running the ink on my Wordsworth essay.

I locked up my bike and waited alone
on the elegant doorstep 'til a woman
in overall and rubber gloves
brought me in across the clean pale carpet,
lifted my sodden coat,
put the unpleasant hat away to dry,
let me shake out tangled hair,
sit on the edge of the sofa.

Mr S was still in the shower.

What I remember best
is that she handed me coffee
in his white translucent china,
more beautiful than I had ever seen,
the cup's shallow bowl
covered in big blue butterflies,
indigo, paint-box, inkblot blue.

Our eyes flickered like accomplices.

Mr S came in, white shirt unbuttoned,
tousled and barefoot, dried and scented,
gazed at my damp red face, my blotchy essay.
I read it out. He went through questions
and answers. I was a slug
in his butterfly garden. Afterwards
I was told I was lucky; he sometimes
came nude to tutorials
or wearing a small white towel
carelessly caught at the navel.

For years I forgot him and worked
on growing more skin.
Then stale news
across hundreds of miles: his death.

One night he met his murderer
who stabbed him in that smart room,
it being his habit to look for strange young men
to use his towels, to touch him and rob him,
to drink from his butterfly china.